STAR WARS™

I Want to be a Jedi

Simon Beecroft

Contents

The Jedi	3		Mind Powers	18
Jedi Training	4		Jedi Equipment	20
Jedi in Training	6		Jedi Pilots	22
Master and Learner	8		Jedi Enemies	25
The Jedi Council	10		Dark Side	26
Lightsabers	12		A New Era	28
Lightsaber Battles	15		Glossary	30
Mind Tricks	16		Index	32

Mace Windu

Obi-Wan Kenobi

The Jedi

If you want to be a Jedi, you must learn all about Jedi ways. The Jedi are the best fighters in the **galaxy** but their job is to keep the peace.

A Jedi trains hard for many years. Then he or she travels around the galaxy to wherever there is trouble. The Jedi do all they can to bring peace without having to fight.

A Jedi learns about a powerful energy field called **the Force**. The Force is everywhere. A Jedi must be able to understand and use the Force.

Yoda

Great Power

You cannot see the Force but you can learn to feel it. Jedi like Yoda use the Force to help others in the galaxy.

Jedi Training

To be a Jedi, you must start your training when you are very young. First you will be a **Youngling**. If you pass your tests, you become a **Padawan Learner**. This means you are training to be a Jedi, but you are not a Jedi yet. If you train hard and pass more tests, you will become a **Jedi Knight**.

Jedi usually go on missions in pairs.

When you are a Padawan you will go on **missions**.
A Jedi Master will always go with you. A Jedi Master
is the most **experienced** Jedi of all. One day,
if you keep training and learning, you too could
become a Jedi Master.

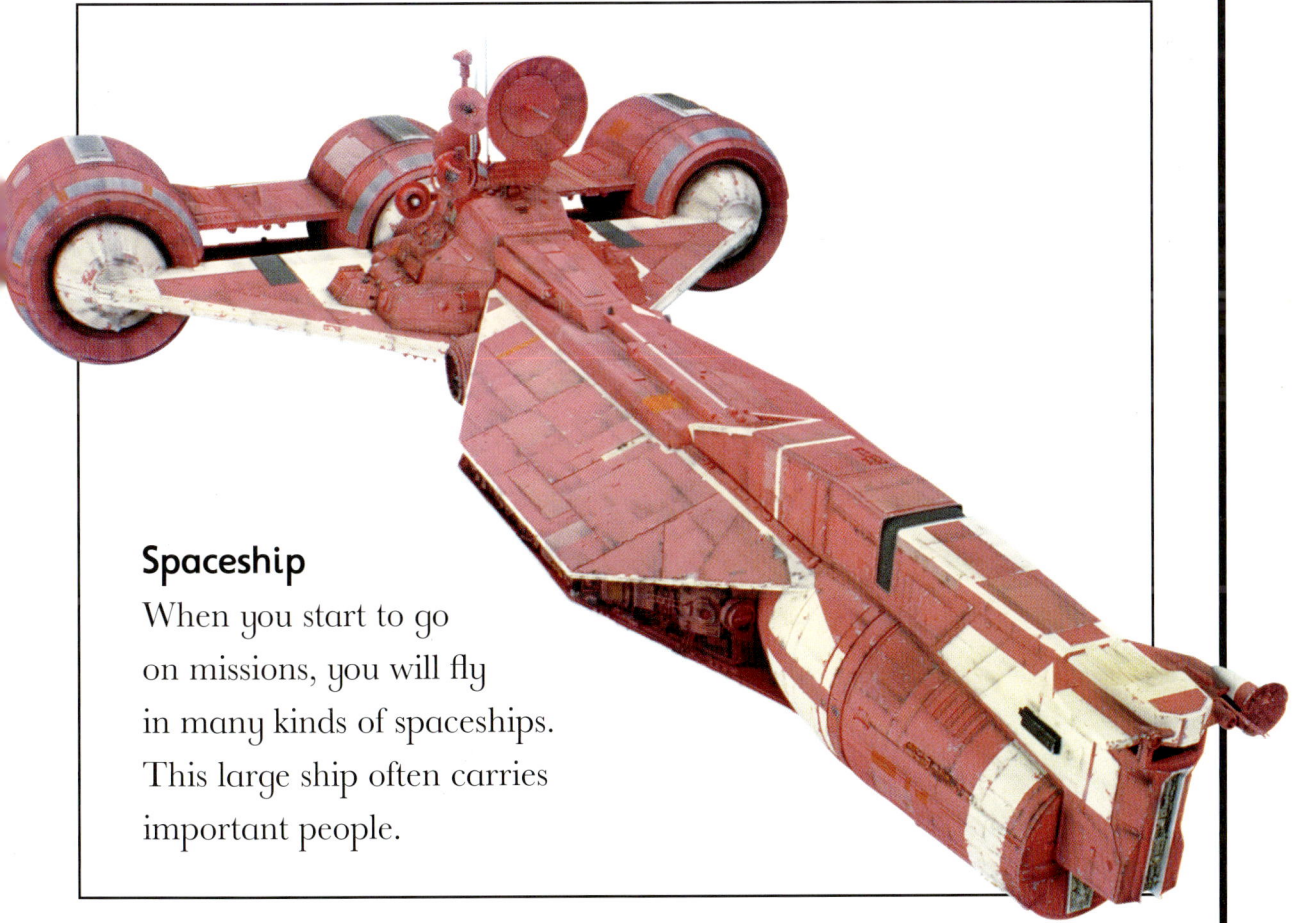

Spaceship

When you start to go
on missions, you will fly
in many kinds of spaceships.
This large ship often carries
important people.

Jedi in Training

When you begin training to be a Jedi you must leave your home, friends and family. So you must really want to be a Jedi.

You travel from your home to a big planet at the centre of the galaxy. A building called the **Jedi Temple** will be your home for the rest of your life. Here is where your Jedi training begins.

A New Home

The Jedi Temple is a huge building where all Jedi live, train and work.

Using special training helmets, Jedi Master Yoda teaches the Younglings how to 'see' without using their eyes.

At the Jedi Temple, you have many classes to learn all the Jedi skills. You learn to **control** your feelings so that you do not feel fear, anger or hate. You learn to use the Force.

Master and Learner

When you are training to be a Jedi, you spend a lot of time with your teacher. Your teacher will be a Jedi Master.

Anakin Skywalker's teacher was called Obi-Wan Kenobi (say: *oh-bee-one ken-oh-bee*). Anakin felt that Obi-Wan was not teaching him fast enough.

Anakin does not always listen to what Obi-Wan Kenobi tells him.

Anakin tells Chancellor Palpatine (say: pal-pa-teen) that Obi-Wan is teaching him too slowly. Anakin believes Palpatine is a good friend.

Anakin could not wait to become a Jedi Knight. He was more powerful than most Jedi but he did not always follow the rules of the **Jedi Order**.

The Jedi Council

The most powerful and wise Jedi sit on the Jedi High Council. These Jedi make very important decisions. Two of the most important members of the Jedi Council are Yoda and Mace Windu.

Yoda is a very wise, green-skinned alien who is many hundreds of years old.

Mace Windu is a human Jedi with great powers of thought. Yoda and Mace are both highly skilled with the Jedi's only weapon, which is called a **lightsaber**.

Mace Windu

Lightsabers

Lightsabers work like swords, but the blade is not made of metal. A lightsaber blade is made of glowing energy that can be many different colours. It is much more powerful than a metal blade, so a Jedi must learn how to use it safely and carefully.

Jedi Master Qui-Gon (say: kwy-gon) protects Queen Amidala from a battle droid.

Jedi must never use their lightsabers to attack others. They must use them only to **defend** and protect.

Jedi build their own lightsabers, so every lightsaber is different. If you lose your lightsaber you must build another one yourself.

Lightsaber handle

You hold your lightsaber by the handle. When you **activate** it, the blade comes out of the end. The blade can cut almost anything.

Lightsaber Battles

The Jedi use their lightsabers to defend themselves and others. Lightsabers can stop objects and blaster fire. They can slice open locked doors with ease.

Sometimes, a Jedi may face an enemy who also uses a lightsaber. When fighting, Jedi use the Force to make their movements faster. They also use the Force to feel what moves the other person will make, even before they have made them.

Jedi Master Qui-Gon fights a deadly enemy called Darth Maul.

Mind Tricks

The Jedi may wave one of their hands, as they suggest a thought to another person. The person doesn't know that the Jedi has put the thought in their mind. This is called a Jedi mind trick.

Jedi mind tricks do not work on everyone. Some people can resist the Jedi mind trick.

All in the Mind

Once Obi-Wan used a Jedi mind trick on a small-time criminal. He convinced the crook to change his ways.

Anakin Skywalker used to be a slave. He was owned by an alien called Watto. Qui-Gon tried to free Anakin by using a mind trick on Watto, but it didn't work.

Mind Powers

Jedi can also use the Force to move objects without touching them. A skilled Jedi can move objects of any size, large or small.

Great Teacher

Yoda taught a young Jedi called Luke Skywalker how to lift heavy objects using the Force.

Wise Jedi like Yoda can lift very heavy objects using their minds. Yoda can move heavy rocks and even lift a spaceship out of a swamp!

Jedi mind powers also help a Jedi in battle. If a Jedi drops his lightsaber, he can quickly make it jump back into his hand using the Force.

Jedi Equipment

The Jedi take special tools with them when they go on a mission. They never know what they might need! They hang their lightsaber on a special belt. The belt also holds a medical kit, tools, food **capsules** and a special communication **device** called a comlink. The Jedi use comlinks to send and receive messages.

Comlink

Qui-Gon uses his comlink to speak with Obi-Wan Kenobi.

Qui-Gon uses his holoprojector to show pictures of a spaceship.

Jedi also use a holoprojector. This lets a Jedi record an image and then play it back later. A holoprojector can also send a moving image of yourself to someone else, like a video link.

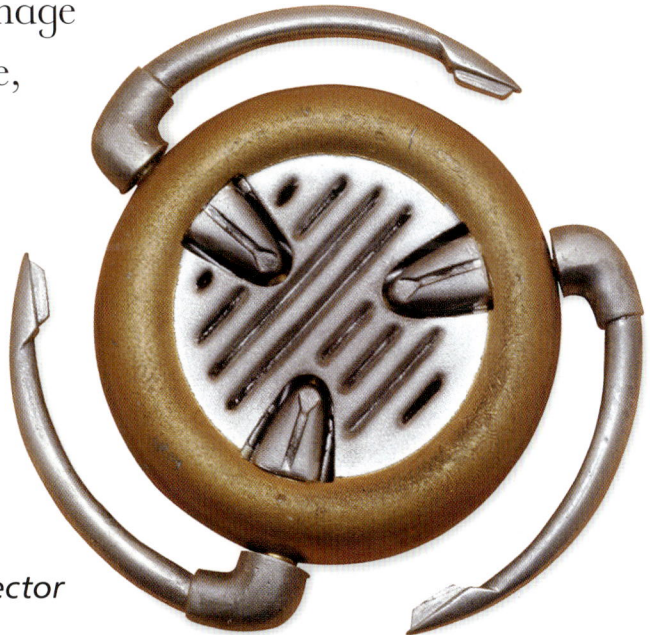

Holoprojector

Jedi Pilots

The Jedi are some of the best pilots in the galaxy. Often they use their Force powers when they are flying spaceships.

Anakin Skywalker can fly at top speed using his Force powers. The Jedi can fly many kinds of **vehicles**, such as flying cars called **airspeeders**.

Anakin uses all his Jedi skills to fly an airspeeder through a city.

Obi-Wan pilots his Jedi starfighter away from danger.

When the Jedi go on missions, they often fly small ships called **starfighters**. There is just enough space for the Jedi pilot and a small **droid**.

Pilot Droids

Pilot droids help Jedi to pilot spaceships. This droid is called R2-D2.

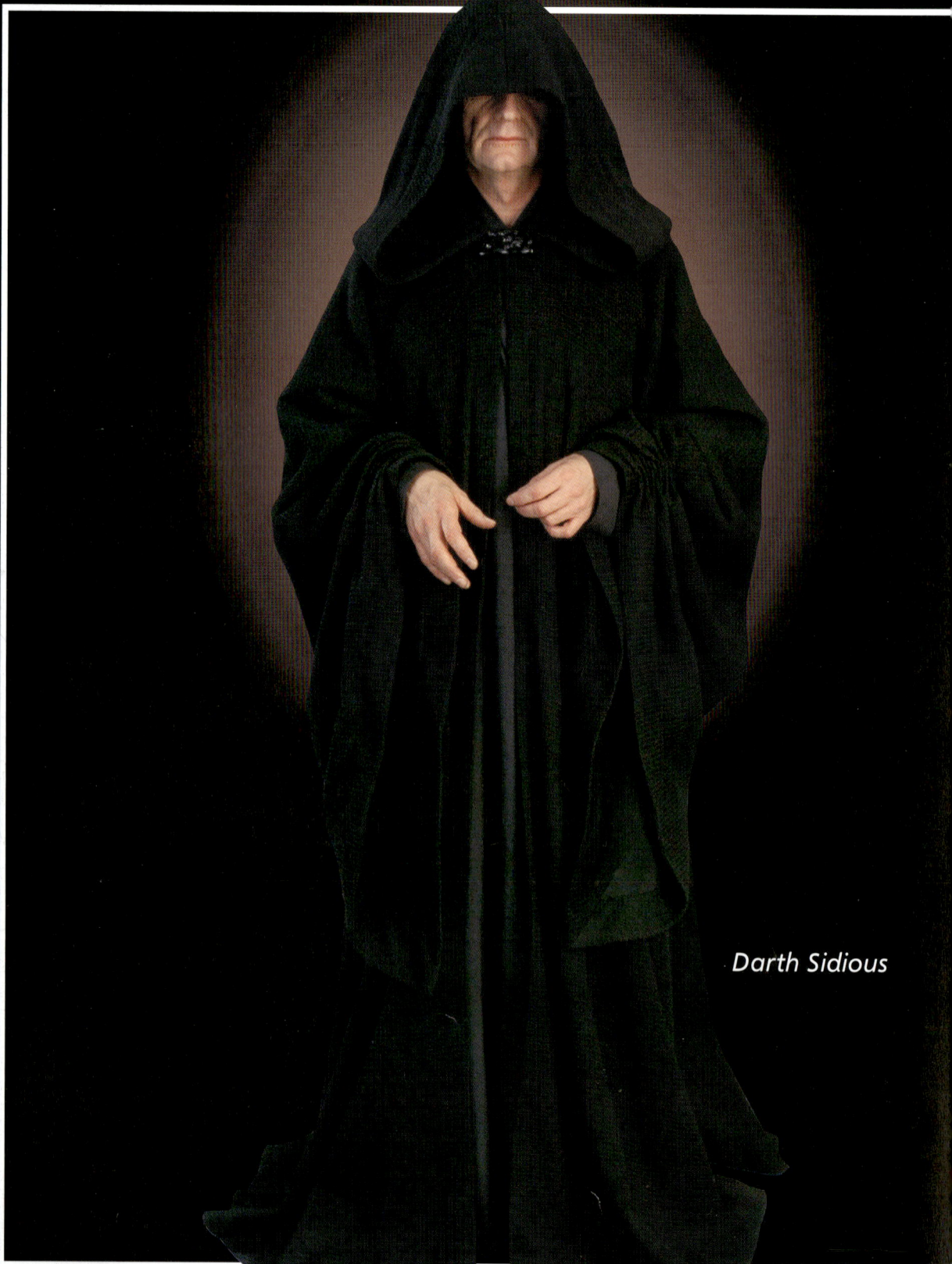

Darth Sidious

Jedi Enemies

The Jedi have powerful enemies called the Sith. The Sith use the **dark side** of the Force to gain powers. The Sith want to destroy the Jedi.

A long time ago, the Sith and the Jedi fought a war. The Jedi thought they defeated the Sith, but one Sith Master survived. This Sith Master secretly trained one other person. For a thousand years, the Sith skills stayed alive.

The final Sith Master was called Darth Sidious (say: *sid-ee-us*). He planned to destroy the Jedi once and for all.

Dark Side

The worst thing a Jedi can do is to turn away from the good side of the Force and begin using the dark side.

One of the most powerful Jedi of all, Anakin Skywalker, turned to the dark side during a war. He joined the evil Sith Darth Sidious and became a Sith.

Anakin killed many Jedi. He even tried to kill his oldest friend and teacher, Obi-Wan. Obi-Wan did not want to fight his old friend, but he had to. It took all his strength and powers, but in the end he thought he had killed Anakin. He was wrong.

A New Era

The war between the Sith and the Jedi was the most dangerous time the galaxy had ever seen. Nearly all of the Jedi died. The evil Sith Lords won the war and ruled the galaxy. Anakin also survived. Now he was called Darth Vader and he wore a black helmet.

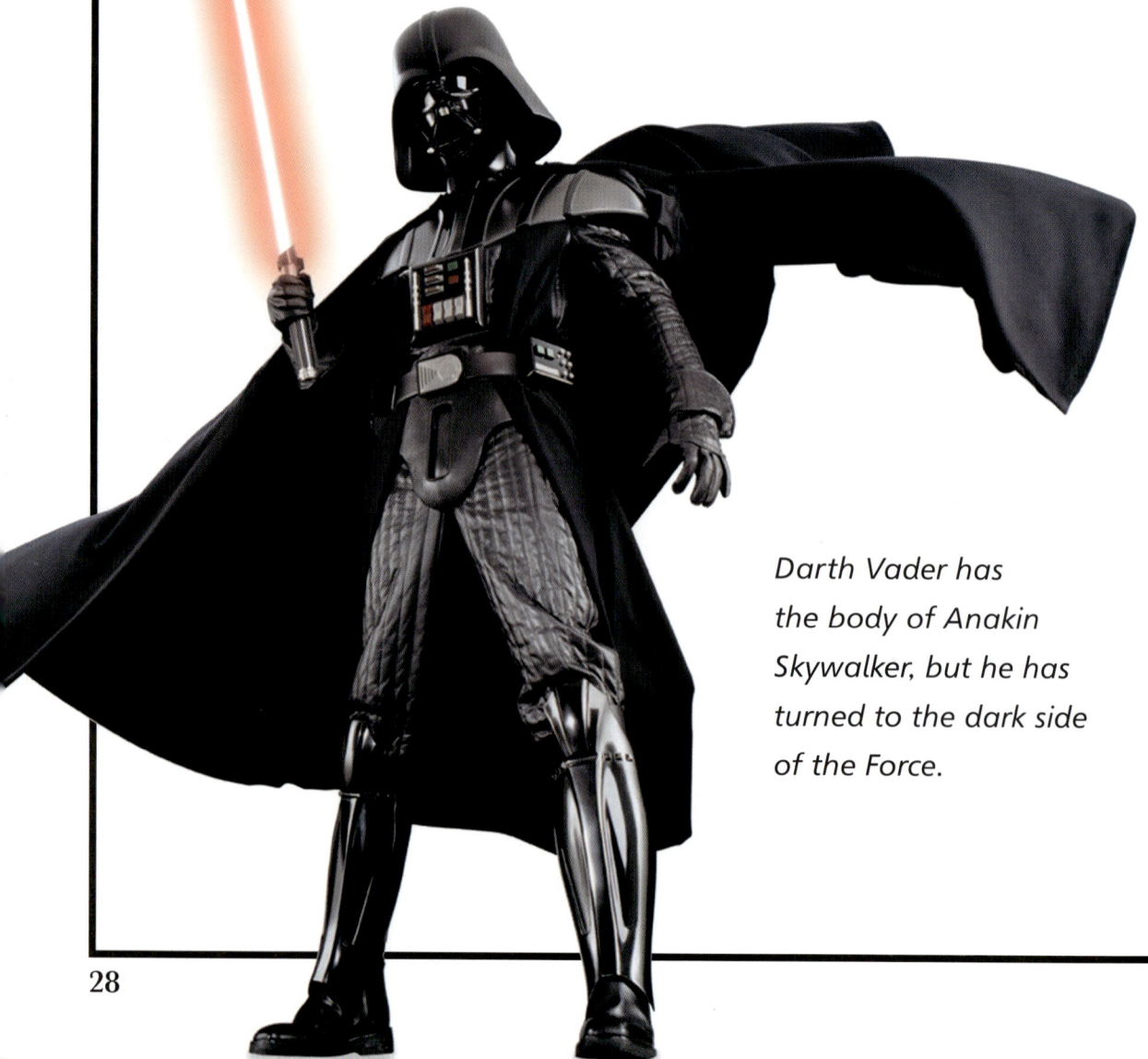

Darth Vader has the body of Anakin Skywalker, but he has turned to the dark side of the Force.

Luke Skywalker never thought he would become a Jedi, but he did.

Obi-Wan Kenobi trained Luke Skywalker to be a Jedi. Luke then helped his father destroy the Sith once and for all.

As long as there are Jedi, there is hope for the galaxy.

May the Force be with you!

Luke Skywalker is the son of Anakin and Padmé.

Glossary

activate
turn something on

airspeeder
type of flying car

control
have power over; have command of

dark side
part of the Force to do with fear and hatred

defend
guard against, protect

device
object, gadget

droid
kind of robot. R2-D2 is a droid.

experienced
wise and very good at something

the Force
energy field created by all living things

galaxy
group of millions of stars and planets

Jedi Knight
Star Wars warrior with special powers who defends the good of the galaxy. Anakin Skywalker, Luke Skywalker and Obi-Wan Kenobi are all Jedi Knights.

Jedi Order
name of a group that defends peace and justice in the galaxy

Jedi Temple
Jedi headquarters where the Jedi Council meets and Jedi live, train and work

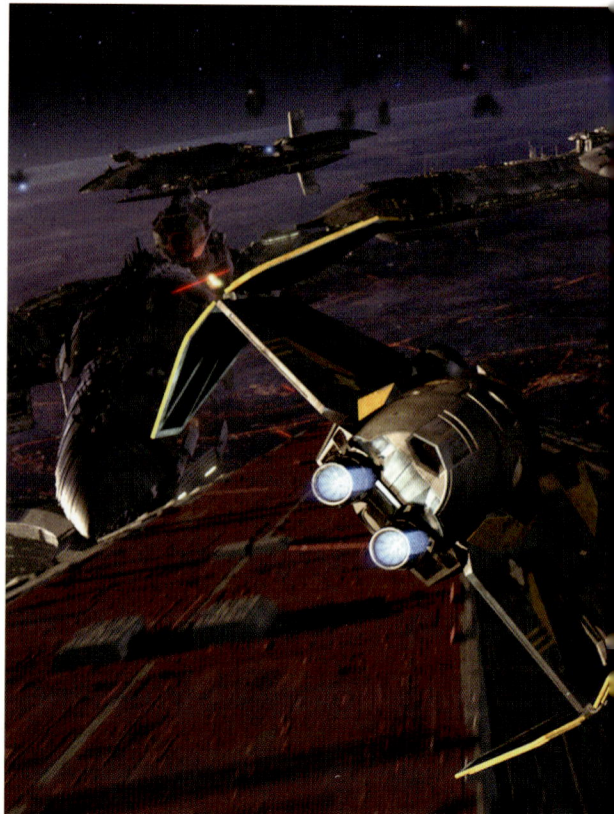

lightsaber
Jedi's and Sith's weapon, made of glowing energy

missions
special tasks or duties

Padawan Learner
Jedi who is learning the ways of the Force

Sith
enemies of the Jedi who use the dark side of the Force

starfighter
small, fast spaceship used by Jedi and others

vehicles
machines used for transport

Youngling
first stage of Jedi training, before you become a Padawan Learner

Index

dark side 25, 26, 28

Darth Sidious 24, 25, 26

Darth Vader 28

droids 23

the Force 3, 7, 15, 19, 22,
25, 26, 29

Jedi Council 10–11

Jedi equipment 20–21

Jedi Knight 4

Jedi Master 5, 7, 8, 12, 15

Jedi Temple 6–7

Jinn, Qui-Gon 12, 14, 17, 21

Kenobi, Obi-Wan 2, 8, 9,
16, 20, 23, 27, 29

lightsabers 12–13, 14–15

mind powers 18–19

mind tricks 16–17

Padawan 4–5

Palpatine 9

pilots 22–23

R2-D2 23

Sith 24–25, 26–27, 28–29

Skywalker, Anakin 8, 9, 17,
22, 26, 27, 28, 29

Skywalker, Luke 19, 29

training 4–5, 6–7, 8

Windu, Mace 2, 10, 11

Yoda 3, 7, 10, 11, 19

Youngling 4, 7